NOTORIOUS AMERICANS AND THEIR TIMES

John Wilkes

BOOTH

and the Civil War

by

STEVE OTFINOSKI

Consulting Editor

RACHEL SEIDMAN
Carleton College

BLACKBIRCH PRESS, INC.
WOODBRIDGE, CONNECTICUT

Published by Blackbirch Press, Inc.
260 Amity Road
Woodbridge, CT 06525

e-mail: staff@blackbirch.com
Web site: www.blackbirch.com

©1999 by Blackbirch Press, Inc.
First Edition

Printed in the United States

10 9 8 7 6 5 4 3 2 1

Library of Congress Cataloging-in-Publication Data

Steven.
es Booth and the Civil War / by Steve Otfinoski. — 1st ed.
cm. — (Notorious Americans)
es bibliographical references (p. 73) and index.
nary: Sets the life story of the man who assassinated Abraham
ainst the backdrop of the Civil War.
1-56711-222-6 (lib. bdg. : alk. paper)
oth, John Wilkes, 1838–1865—Juvenile literature. 2. Lincoln, Abraham, 1809–1865—Assassination—Juvenile literature. 3. Assassins—United States—Biography—Juvenile literature. 4. United States—History—Civil War, 1861–1865—Juvenile literature. [1. Booth, John Wilkes, 1838–1865. 2. Lincoln, Abraham, 1809–1865—Assassination. 3. Assassins. 4. United States—History—Civil War, 1861–1865] I. Title.
E457.5.O84   1999
973.7'092—dc21

98-11571
CIP
AC

Table of Contents

Chapter 1

THE NATION'S EARLY YEARS
BOOTH MAKES HIS DEBUT

$\mathcal{T}$he 50 years following the birth of the United States was a time of rapid growth, and often, a period of great optimism. But the new nation was not at peace with itself. Americans were divided over a number of issues. The most bitter disagreements were over slavery, which was practiced in the South but eventually was shunned in the North. By 1861, all hope of a peaceful resolution was gone. The southern states seceded from the Union, and the nation was plunged into the Civil War.

In the course of the four-year war, over 500,000 Americans died. It was a huge death toll for a country of 31 million people. After the North won the war in 1865, the two sides formed one whole nation again.

The man who is given the most credit for preserving the Union was President Abraham Lincoln. He dedicated himself

Opposite: *Harriet Tubman led about 300 slaves to freedom on the Underground Railroad between 1850 and 1860.*

completely to this cause, until he was assassinated on April 14, 1865. His killer was John Wilkes Booth, an actor from Maryland who abandoned a successful career in order to pursue the president. Booth did not care about the divisive issue of slavery as much as some southerners did. But he was convinced that he had to murder Lincoln in order to save the South.

Slavery in the American Colonies

The first African slaves arrived in Jamestown, Virginia, in 1619. Over the next century, slavery spread throughout the American colonies. Gradually, however, the country's three distinct regions—the New England colonies, middle colonies, and southern colonies—began to change in their needs for slaves. As a result, their attitudes toward slavery changed as well.

Slaves were not necessary in the New England colonies (Massachusetts, Connecticut, Rhode Island, and New Hampshire). There the soil was poor, and farms were small enough to be run by family members. Many New Englanders turned away from farming for their living and took up fishing, trading, and manufacturing. Slaves had no training or experience that enabled them to help with these endeavors.

The middle colonies (New York, New Jersey, Pennsylvania, and Delaware) had better soil than New England. Farmers raised large cash crops, such as wheat and corn, that could be sold elsewhere. Many slaves were put to work on huge estate farms, especially in New York's Hudson River Valley.

The southern colonies (Maryland, Virginia, North Carolina, South Carolina, and Georgia) were dependent on slave labor. Large farms, called plantations, produced rice, tobacco, and later, cotton. The slaves who worked the plantations were not paid wages. This meant that their masters earned a greater

profit than they would if they employed paid workers. It should
be noted, though, that while plantations were an important part
of the southern economy, there were many small farms with no
slaves, or only a few.

Manufacturing, which was growing in the New England and
middle colonies, was practically nonexistent in the southern
ones. The South got most of its manufactured goods from
England, and it paid for these goods by selling southern crops
to the English.

The Debate over Slavery

Slavery gradually withered away in New England in the early
1800s. The institution was also greatly reduced in the middle,
or mid-Atlantic, states, where manufacturing and other businesses
replaced agriculture in importance. In the South, however, slavery became more and more essential to an agricultural society.

As slavery disappeared from the North, the people in this
region began to question the whole idea of slavery as an institution. Many thought that it didn't belong in a free country. The
slavery issue seemed urgent in 1787, when the new nation
formed its Constitution. Since the southern states refused to give
up their slaves, northerners agreed to allow slavery to continue
for the good of the nation. But the conflict did not go away.

In the early 1800s, settlers moved west and established communities in new territories. When these territories applied to be
admitted into the Union as states, there was disagreement about
whether they should be admitted as "free" states, where slavery
would be illegal, or as "slave states," where slavery would be
permitted. The issue came to a head in 1819, when Missouri
asked to be admitted to the Union as a slave state. At that time,
there were 11 free states and 11 slave states. Missouri threatened
to upset the balance of power in the legislature, giving slave

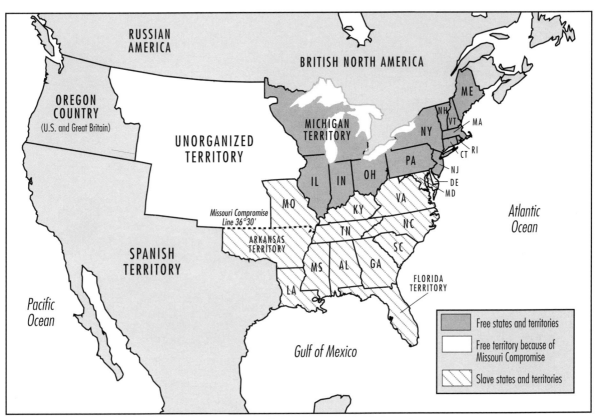

The United States in 1820, at the time of the Missouri Compromise.

states a majority. The following year, an agreement was reached. Under the Missouri Compromise, Missouri was admitted as a slave state, and Maine, which was also applying for statehood, was admitted as a free state. Most important, the compromise banned slavery from all territory north of 36°30' north latitude— a line that forms the southern boundary of Missouri.

While slavery continued to be a controversial issue, there were others that divided the North from the South. One was the question of how strong the federal government should be. The industrial North felt that a strong federal government was needed to impose protective tariffs (taxes) on foreign goods.

By making these goods more expensive, the government helped promote the sale of American products. The new territories of the West needed the help of the federal government in order to establish new communities. The government gave lands to homesteaders, and contributed money for the construction of new roads and railroad lines.

The southern states had a very different viewpoint. They saw little that was good about the federal government. They simply wanted it to leave them alone to pursue their quiet agricultural existence.

The Booth Family

Maryland was one of the northernmost slave-owning states, which were also called the Border States. Among Maryland's most distinguished residents was Junius Brutus Booth. A celebrated Shakespearean actor, he had left his native England to come to the United States in 1821. His dramatic style of acting made him extremely popular in his adopted country. Eventually, he settled in Maryland's Harford County, where he bought a farmhouse near the town of Bel Air.

Junius Booth's private life seemed to mirror his tragic stage roles. He was a notorious alcoholic and suffered brief periods of depression. But he was also very attached to his family. He and his wife, Mary Ann Holmes Booth, had ten children, six of whom survived to adulthood.

The ninth child, John Wilkes, was born May 10, 1838, on the family farm. John was a handsome boy, but he was not as intelligent as his older brothers Edwin and Junius, Jr.

"He had to plod, progress slowly step by step, but that which he once attained he never lost," wrote his sister Asia many years later in a memoir about her brother. "His feelings were ardent and impulsive; in a moment of devotion or enthusiasm he would grant or give anything he possessed." Booth's strong feelings and his tendency to act impulsively would eventually lead him to commit murder.

Western Expansion Sparks Conflicts

While young John Wilkes Booth was starting school in 1846, a war broke out between the United States and Mexico. The war was over the Mexican provinces of New Mexico and California, which the United States originally offered to buy, and Mexico wanted to keep. These provinces included present-day Arizona, Utah, Nevada, and part of Colorado, in addition to California and New Mexico.

Junius Brutus Booth

When American forces invaded the disputed territory and fighting broke out, the United States declared war on Mexico. In 1848, the United States won the war and, as part of the peace settlement, gained the provinces of California and New Mexico. Then the nation faced the dilemma of whether the new territory should be free or slave.

The Wilmot Proviso, a provision of the American peace negotiations with Mexico, declared that slavery would be forbidden in any new territories won from Mexico. The Senate, which was controlled by the South, refused to approve the Proviso. It was resubmitted unsuccessfully to Congress several times, intensifying the conflict between the North and South.

The Fugitive Slave Act

In 1850, an agreement called the Compromise of 1850 was finally approved by Congress. California would be admitted as a free state. But the status of the other lands won from Mexico would be decided when they applied for statehood.

The Compromise of 1850 established a very strict Fugitive Slave Act. According to this act, anyone who came in contact with a runaway slave was legally required to return that slave to his or her master or suffer heavy fines and possible imprisonment.

Many northerners were opposed to the Fugitive Slave Act, including the abolitionists. They were northern radicals—both white and black—who called for an immediate end to slavery in the United States. "We must trample this law under our feet," said abolitionist Wendell Phillips regarding the Fugitive Slave Act. The people who were most opposed to the act were, of course, the slaves themselves. Many decided to try and escape to Canada.

The abolitionists were hated by southerners, and they were not popular with many northerners, either. Most northerners were opposed to slavery, but they wanted to end it gradually. In the meantime, they thought slavery should only be allowed in the South. These moderate northerners viewed the abolitionists as dangerous radicals who could divide the Union and even lead the country into a civil war.

Among the moderates was Abraham Lincoln, a U.S. representative from Illinois, who supported the Wilmot Proviso. Many of the voters in Lincoln's voting district were discouraged by his anti-slavery stand and his opposition to the Mexican War. Realizing he could not win re-election, Lincoln served out his term in the House. In 1849, he quietly returned to his law practice in Springfield, Illinois. Over the next few years he established himself as one of the state's leading lawyers.

Despite its name, the "Underground Railroad" was neither underground nor a railroad. It was an escape route to the North for thousands of runaway slaves.

Between 1830 and 1860, approximately 75,000 slaves escaped the South, "riding" northward on the Underground Railroad. The railroad "tracks" were the back roads and trails the slaves traveled, mostly at night. The "conductors" were the people—both black and white—who provided them with food, clothing, and hiding places called "stations."

Among the most famous of these conductors was Harriet Tubman, who was herself a runaway slave. She risked recapture many times, personally leading about 300 slaves to freedom. Her courage and determination earned her the title "the Moses of her people." (In Biblical times Moses freed the Jews, who were slaves in Egypt.)

Most of the runaways did not "get off" the railroad in the northern states, where they could be recaptured and returned to their masters. They continued on into Canada, where slavery was forbidden and the Fugitive Slave Act did not apply.

Southerners grew to hate the Underground Railroad and the people who operated it. But their threats and the imprisonment of the railroad's conductors did not stop its work. It took a war to do that.

An Actor Is Born

While Lincoln was back in Illinois, young John Wilkes Booth was also facing failure. His father died in 1852 after drinking poisonous water on a Mississippi steamboat. He had been returning home from a theatrical tour. In death, he left his family with a mountain of debts.

The Booth family was forced to rent out the fine Baltimore home they had been living in for years and return to the family farm near Bel Air.

John finished his schooling and moved back home with his mother, two sisters, and younger brother. He tried his hand at farming, but he had neither the temperament nor talent to be a farmer. He referred to his efforts as "trying to starve respectably by torturing the barren earth."

John Wilkes Booth in a Colonial costume

He envied his brothers Junius and Edwin; both had followed their father's example and taken up acting careers. Edwin was quickly becoming one of the country's leading tragedians (actors who play tragic roles). Junius was on his way to becoming a top theatrical manager.

If the theater was in his brothers' blood, John Wilkes felt it must be in his, too. In August 1855, his brothers were acting in a special performance of Shakespeare's *Richard III* at the Charles Street Theater in Baltimore. John Wilkes was cast in a supporting role.

His performance was weak, but the critics were kind to him because of his legendary father. Booth mistook their generosity for genuine praise. When he arrived home, he was very excited. "His face shone with enthusiasm," wrote Asia, "and given the exultant tone of his voice it was plain that he had passed the test night." Booth decided that he, too, would become an actor.

In his first stage role Booth played Richmond, the hero who killed the tyrant Richard III and freed England from Richard's reign of terror. It was a role that Booth would one day aspire to play in real life, with tragic consequences for his country.

Chapter 2

AN ILLINOIS SENATOR IN WASHINGTON

THE ACTOR'S STAR RISES

*I*n 1859, on the morning of December 2, the 59-year-old abolitionist John Brown went to his execution at Harpers Ferry, Virginia. Many witnesses were amazed at Brown's calm manner. Among those present was 21-year-old John Wilkes Booth, a member of the Virginia militia.

Booth was deeply committed to the South, and he had little patience for abolitionists. "I saw John Brown hung," he later wrote, "…and while I live, I shall think with joy upon the day when I saw the sun go down upon one traitor less within our land."

The reasons Booth and Brown were in Harpers Ferry on that cold December day had to do with the nation's deep divisions over the burning issue of slavery.

"Bleeding Kansas"

As more western territories clamored to become part of the United States, the South expressed its dissatisfaction with the arbitrary "slave line" established during the Missouri Compromise. Two of these new territories were Kansas and Nebraska, which were former Native American lands. In order to settle the growing dispute over whether Kansas and Nebraska would be free or slave states, Democratic Senator Stephen A. Douglas of Illinois proposed a bill. According to this bill, which became the Kansas-Nebraska Act of 1854, the question of slavery would be settled in each new territory by the people living there. This move toward "popular sovereignty," or rule by the people, was seen as fair and democratic by southerners and by northern moderates like Douglas. But northerners who were strongly opposed to slavery saw the act as a betrayal, and they refused to support it.

The debate in Congress over the Kansas-Nebraska Act was long and intense. President Franklin Pierce, who grew up in the abolitionist stronghold of New Hampshire, shocked many northerners by supporting the bill. With his help, the Kansas-Nebraska Act eventually became law.

Instead of soothing the fears of the North and South, the Kansas-Nebraska Act increased them. Kansas, which had ardent supporters both for and against slavery, became a living symbol of the national conflict. In the election of 1855, pro-slavery candidates won a majority of the seats in the new state legislature, and they passed laws favoring slavery. Violence broke out between those who were in favor of slavery and those who opposed it, earning the territory a grim nickname—"Bleeding Kansas."

Among the most radical abolitionists in Kansas was the failed businessman John Brown, who settled in Osawatomie, in the eastern part of the state, in 1855. When pro-slavery men attacked

In the nation's capital, the slavery issue was debated in the U.S. Supreme Court as well as in Congress. In 1857, the Supreme Court handed down the *Dred Scott* decision. Scott was a slave and personal servant to a U.S. army surgeon. In 1834, he traveled with his master from Missouri, where slavery was legal, to Illinois and the Wisconsin Territory, where it was not.

After the death of his master in 1846, Scott sued his master's widow for his freedom. He argued that he had lived in both a free state and territory for four years, and should rightly be freed.

Scott was granted his freedom by a local Missouri court, but that decision was reversed by the state supreme court. The case finally came before the U.S. Supreme Court in 1857. The justices ruled that slaves were not citizens and had no basic rights. Instead, they were personal property, and would remain the property of their masters wherever they were taken. The court further ruled that the Missouri Compromise was unconstitutional and that Congress had no right to prohibit slavery in any U.S. territory.

Northerners who opposed slavery were furious. Southerners claimed that their opinion on slavery "is now the supreme law of the land."

Although it was a major setback for the North, the *Dred Scott* decision stiffened northern resolve against slavery. Some states even made their own laws to protect runaway slaves.

---

the anti-slavery community of Lawrence the following May and burned it to the ground, Brown promised vengeance. With a group of followers, he hunted down and brutally murdered five pro-slavery settlers in Osawatomie.

This was only the beginning of Brown's violent tactics. He believed the fight against slavery had to be carried into the South itself. Brown started to collect arms and volunteers for a full-scale invasion.

The Raid on Harpers Ferry

On October 16, 1859, Brown and 18 followers descended on the federal arsenal, where arms were stored at Harpers Ferry, Virginia. His plan was to take all the weapons in the arsenal and head for

Federal troops crash through the door of the railroad roundhouse and capture John Brown.

the countryside. There he would provide slaves with enough guns for a bloody rebellion. But the plan quickly came apart. The people of Harpers Ferry fought back, and Brown took some of them as hostages. Brown and his hostages were trapped in a railroad roundhouse, where locomotives were stored. Within two days, federal troops led by Colonel Robert E. Lee arrived. Edward White, a teacher, described the final moments of the siege as the soldiers stormed the roundhouse:

> *Once-Twice- the impromptu battering ram thundered upon the door. Suddenly there was a tremendous crash and a fragment of the door some two and one half feet wide, and extending from top to bottom, was hurled in upon the defenders.*

JOHN WILKES BOOTH AND THE CIVIL WAR

In less time than I can attempt to tell it, the motionless figure of Lieutenant Green [commander of the band of soldiers] *sprang into life. He leaped through the breach, followed by his men. Fortunately for him his foot tripped on the tongue of the engine or hose carriage, and he fell. At that moment, Brown himself fired; but the ball intended for Green, struck the unfortunate Marine who followed, and he lived but a few hours.*

Booth later claimed he was among the soldiers who captured Brown, but there is little historical evidence to support this statement. He was at the hanging, however, probably as a member of the Militia Company F of Richmond Volunteers, a group he had joined only a short time earlier.

Booth's feelings toward John Brown, who was condemned for treason and murder, were somewhat confused. On one hand, he saw the abolitionist as a black-hearted villain who deserved to die for what he had done. But Booth could not help but admire Brown's uncompromising stand against slavery, and his willingness to die for a cause.

Northerners were equally divided in their opinions of John Brown. While many condemned his actions, his dignified manner during his trial won him the admiration of those who shared his hatred of slavery. The New England writer Ralph Waldo Emerson praised him as "a saint [who] would make the gallows glorious like the Cross."

"A Southern Actor"

Booth's decision to join the militia was a natural extension of his growing love for the South and its cause of slavery. His affection increased even as he continued to purse an acting career.

Booth in street clothes

After his debut on the stage in 1855, he signed on as an apprentice actor with the company of the Arch Street Theatre in Philadelphia. He billed himself as "J. Wilkes," hoping to succeed on his own merits without the family name.

Booth's progress was slow. In early performances, he forgot his lines, acted too dramatically, or became paralyzed by stage fright. Several times he was booed and hissed off the stage. Despite these setbacks, he worked at his craft. As he gained confidence, he showed the same dramatic flair that had made his father a popular stage actor.

In 1858, Booth joined the Marshall Theater company in Richmond, the capital of Virginia. The elegance of the city's gentry—Virginia's most wealthy and refined people—appealed to Booth. They, in turn, admired Booth's handsome appearance and magnetic personality. The young actor quickly became the darling of Richmond society. For two years he remained there, playing increasingly important roles and winning audiences' hearts, especially the hearts of young women. His sister observed that "he wanted to be loved of the Southern people above all things. He would work to make himself eventually a Southern actor."

But the greater stage of the real world also attracted Booth. He identified with the South and its way of life and deeply resented the interference of northerners who wanted to change it. In a reckless moment, he joined the militia to bind himself more closely to his southern brothers. Booth's passion for being a soldier faded quickly, however. Soon after he saw John Brown's execution, Booth left the militia.

When asked why he didn't join the Confederate army when the Civil War erupted, he replied that he had promised his mother not to enter in the fighting. Some historians have said he had an unnatural fear of having his handsome face scarred in battle. Whatever the reason, John Wilkes Booth would never play a soldier again, except on a stage.

Lincoln for President

Abraham Lincoln was as awkward and physically unappealing as Booth was athletic and dashing. Although he did not wish to radically change the South and its way of life, Lincoln believed slavery was morally wrong. He felt that it should not be allowed in the new territories. Lincoln was a strong opponent of the Kansas-Nebraska Act and of the man who had proposed it—Stephen Douglas.

In 1856, Lincoln joined the newly formed Republican party, which was anti-slavery. He campaigned energetically for the party's

Abraham Lincoln ran for the Senate in 1858.

first Presidential candidate, John C. Fremont. Although Fremont lost the election, the favorable public attention that Lincoln received during the campaign made him a rising star in the Republican party. In 1858, he became the Republican party's candidate for U.S. senator from the state of Illinois. Lincoln's opponent was Stephen Douglas.

The Lincoln-Douglas debates were the among the most remarkable and eloquent political discussions in American history. While both candidates were opposed to the idea of slavery, Douglas saw it as a political issue that required compromise. Lincoln saw slavery as an evil that eventually had to be removed from American life. In one famous speech he claimed "this government cannot endure, permanently half *slave* and half *free*." Douglas won the election, but Lincoln emerged as a leading national spokesperson for his party.

When the Republican party met in Chicago in May 1860 to nominate a candidate for president, Lincoln was one of the men under consideration. Other potential candidates were more experienced and powerful, but Lincoln had other advantages. He was a fresh face, and his humble upbringing in a log cabin was sure to appeal to voters. In addition, Lincoln had few enemies. He seemed to be an excellent compromise candidate who could unite the Republican party. Lincoln won the nomination, distressing many southern Democrats, who saw his possible election as a threat to everything the South stood for.

The Democrats were deeply divided over the slavery issue. Douglas became the candidate of the northern Democrats, and Vice-President John C. Breckenridge, of the southern Democrats. The two candidates split the Democratic vote, and Lincoln won the election in November. Several southern states had threatened to secede from the Union if Lincoln was elected, and on December 20, 1860, South Carolina did just that.

About the same time, John Wilkes Booth visited his family in Pennsylvania for the Christmas holidays. He was fresh from his first tour as a starring player. At age 21, he was celebrated as an actor who could follow in his famous father's footsteps.

But John Wilkes Booth was as preoccupied with the state of the nation as he was with his acting career. In the last days of 1860, he sat down to write a remarkable 20-page speech filled with the pain and anguish he felt for the South and his resentment of the newly elected president, Abraham Lincoln. It was a speech he would never deliver, but the words became a part of his very being.

> *I am a northern man. But unlike most Northerners, I have looked upon both sides of this question.... I will not fight for secession.... But I will fight with all my heart and should, even if there's not a man to back me, for equal rights and justice to the South.*

Booth, like John Brown, had taken his position, and he would stand by it to the end.

Chapter 3

THE THEATER OF WAR

A KIDNAPPING IS PLANNED

One evening in early 1861, an unusual admirer appeared backstage to meet John Wilkes Booth after his performance in a Richmond theater. The man was a simple southerner who was not very well educated. Yet there was an earnestness and sincerity to Lewis Powell that impressed Booth. The feeling was mutual.

"Each was what the other was not," wrote Louis J. Weichmann, an acquaintance of Booth's who later wrote a book about him. "The actor was pleased to have a follower so powerful in his muscles and Powell was irresistibly drawn to follow a man so wonderful fascinating and intellectual."

Booth and Powell formed an unlikely friendship and, in time, Powell would follow his hero farther than either ever dreamed of at the time.

The Fighting Starts

Lewis Powell's home state was Florida. It was one of six states that followed South Carolina's lead and seceded from the Union by the time Lincoln was inaugurated in March 1861. The others were Mississippi, Alabama, Georgia, Louisiana, and Texas. The month before Lincoln's inauguration, representatives of all seven states met in Montgomery, Alabama, and established themselves as the Confederate States of America, also known as the Confederacy. They elected Jefferson Davis as their president, and chose Richmond, Virginia, to be their capital.

One of the Confederacy's first plans of action was to seize federal forts within their borders. Among the most important of these military outposts was Fort Sumter, in the harbor of Charleston, South Carolina. When supplies ran low at Fort Sumter, President Lincoln wisely sent only necessary provisions, and not troops. But in spite of Lincoln's caution, South Carolina called his action an act of aggression and demanded the surrender of Major Robert Anderson, commander of Fort Sumter. Anderson refused, and on April 12, Confederate artillery fired on the fort from shore. The next day, Anderson surrendered.

Lewis Powell

While soldiers on both sides were fighting and dying on battlefields, many people in the North were actually profiting from the Civil War. Industries such as iron and steel provided the weapons for war. Farmers earned large profits selling grain and other produce to the government to feed the soldiers. Factories ran day and night making clothing and shoes for the army. New inventions such as the sewing machine increased wartime production. Employment was at an all-time high, and mills and factories hired tens of thousands of workers.

But not everyone was happy. As the ranks of volunteers grew smaller, the federal government enacted draft laws that forced young men to join the army. The government excused those who could pay $300 to hire a substitute, however.

In July 1863, the frustrations of poor, ordinary people who had to fight resulted in mob violence in New York. During the "Draft Riots," as they were called, armed mobs took over sections of the city and set them ablaze. Eventually, the army was called in to restore order. The rioters killed many blacks, blaming them for the war.

The South experienced few such incidents, even though southerners suffered economically. Factories in the South were not equipped to turn out all the goods that were needed. Before the war, the South imported clothing and many household items from Europe. Now these imports could not get through the Union naval blockade. Southerners had to make do with what they had. With their menfolk off fighting, many southern women bravely ran their households. They fed their families the foods they managed to grow and sewed curtains and drapes into clothing. Southern women did not always suffer quietly, however. In Richmond, Virginia, they rioted for food because prices were so outrageously high.

Women in the North ran farms and businesses while their husbands were away, just as Southern women did. They also raised million of dollars for the Union army through ladies aid societies, and they sent the soldiers food, medicine, and clothing. And northern women worked as nurses, bringing better sanitation to military hospitals.

President Lincoln immediately called for a blockade of all southern ports, which would cut them off from supplies. After decades of compromises, debate, and accommodation, the dreaded Civil War had begun.

At first, the North thought it could easily win the war within several months. Thousands of volunteers signed up to fight so as not to miss the glory of the few short battles that would surely bring the South to its knees.

New York's "Draft Riots" were so violent that the army was called in to restore peace.

The Battle of Bull Run

On July 21, 1861, Union forces led by General Irvin McDowell met Confederate troops under General P.G.T. Beauregard at Manassas Junction, Virginia. Southerners, who named their battles after townships, called it the battle of Manassas. Northerners, more partial to bodies of water, called it the battle of Bull Run, after a local stream. By whatever name, it was a major engagement.

At first it looked as if the North would take the day as McDowell's troops drove the Confederates back to a stone bridge that crossed Bull Run. But Confederate General Thomas J. Jackson refused to move. He held back the Union advance long enough for another Confederate brigade to arrive and put the fight on an equal footing.

Now it was the Union's turn to fall back. The retreat quickly turned into a major defeat as the inexperienced Union soldiers fled for the safety of Washington. The Confederates, equally inexperienced, failed to pursue them. The South rejoiced in this unexpected victory. The North realized the war would not be a summer affair. And the Confederate general who stubbornly held on and won the day would be forever known as "Stonewall" Jackson.

A Star of the First Magnitude

The war did not end America's need for entertainment. In fact, the theater was more popular than ever. A good production was a welcome diversion that took people's minds off the grimness of war. Even President Lincoln found time in his busy schedule to enjoy an evening at the theater once in a while.

The poet Walt Whitman found the theatrical productions of the era superficial and silly. He was amazed that Lincoln, "the leading actor in the greatest and stormiest drama known to real history's stage…should sit there and be so completely interested and absorbed in these human jackstraws."

Like their president, many Americans were fond of the theater. Among the actors most adored by the public was John Wilkes Booth. "The Pride of the American People," boasted one theatre program about Booth's performance in Shakespeare's *Richard III*.

A popular leading man, Booth was adored by theatergoers in the 1850's and early 1860's.

Despite his intense focus on his successful acting career, Booth never lost his passion for the southern cause. The outbreak of the Civil War only intensified his protective feelings for the homeland he had adopted.

While many of his colleagues in the theatre did not take Booth's angry talk against the North very seriously, he was actually backing his words with deeds. He bought medical supplies and smuggled them across the battle lines to southern hospitals, where they were desperately needed. He also smuggled information to Confederate scouts. (Historians do not know how Booth acquired this information, or how valuable it was.)

Bloody Antietam

While Booth was looking for a grander way to serve the South, the Confederate commander in chief, Robert E. Lee, was trying to do the same by achieving a military victory on northern soil. Such a victory, southern leaders felt, would make their struggle seem more important in the world's eyes and gain them both recognition and aid from Europe, especially from Great Britain.

Lee invaded Maryland in September 1862 and proceeded to Sharpsburg, taking up a position along Antietam Creek. It was here that Union commander General George McClellan came upon Lee's troops on September 17.

The battle of Antietam was the single bloodiest day of the Civil War. The dead and wounded on both sides totaled about 23,000. The North officially won, but it was not a joyous victory. Lee's invasion had been stopped, but McClellan, never an aggressive fighter, let the Confederates get away to fight another day.

Lincoln was disappointed with his commander and relieved McClellan from command for the second time. But his next two commanders did not do much better during two confrontations

Union soldiers storm the bridge at Antietam.

in Virginia. General Ambrose Burnside was defeated at the battle of Fredericksburg in December 1862, and Joseph ("Fighting Joe") Hooker was thoroughly beaten by Lee at the battle of Chancellorsville in May 1863.

Slavery Is Abolished

Lincoln did not restrict the North's struggle against slavery to the battlefield. He was also fighting against the institution in a political arena. On January 1, 1863, President Lincoln signed the Emancipation Proclamation, freeing all slaves in territories controlled by the rebels. The idea for this bold move was not entirely Lincoln's. Prominent black leaders in the North, such as the abolitionist Frederick Douglass, had been urging the president to free the slaves for quite some time.

When Lincoln issued the proclamation, it was a grand gesture that had little immediate effect. The Confederacy did not acknowledge Lincoln's authority, and slaves in border states were not affected. (The president did not free the slaves in border states because he dared not offend these states and lose their critical support.) The Emancipation Proclamation did isolate the South further from the rest of the country, however, and it put a mark of shame on the practice of slavery.

The Greatest Battle

In the summer of 1863, the war reached a critical point. Encouraged by his victory at Chancellorsville, Lee made his second advance into northern territory—this time, into Pennsylvania. He was pursued by Union troops led by General George Meade. The two massive armies met quite by accident in the countryside surrounding the quiet town of Gettysburg. The fighting lasted three full days, from July 1 to July 3, and proved to be the largest battle ever waged in the Western Hemisphere. About 90,000 Union soldiers clashed with 75,000 Confederates.

On the third day, Confederate General George Pickett led 15,000 troops up a high spot called Cemetery Ridge in an

In July 1863, the Union won an important victory at the battle of Gettysburg.

attempt to force Union troops from that strategic position. Lieutenant Frank Haskell, a Union officer, described the scene from where he stood:

> *More than half a mile their front extends; more than a thousand yards the dull gray masses deploy, man touching man, rank pressing rank, and line supporting line. The red flags wave, their horsemen gallop up and down; the arms of eighteen thousand men, barrel and bayonet, gleam in the sun, a sloping forest of flashing steel.*

THE THEATER OF WAR: A KIDNAPPING IS PLANNED

The Confederates took the ridge, but their victory was over in a matter of minutes. They were quickly pushed back under heavy artillery attack from the defending Union troops. "Pickett's Charge" became a symbol of the spirit and bravery of the South, but also a sign of its doomed fate.

About 50,000 soldiers died during the three-day battle. It finally ended with Lee's withdrawal toward Virginia on the night of July 4. Meade failed to take advantage of the situation, and he did not pursue the enemy, just as McClellan had failed to do at Antietam.

Nevertheless, the battle was a crushing defeat for the South. The Confederacy remained on the defensive after Gettysburg, and never advanced so far north again.

Gettysburg was not the only great Union victory during that eventful week. In Mississippi, General Ulysses S. Grant won the city of Vicksburg in a fierce battle. It was the latest in a string of Grant's victories in the West. Lincoln had finally found a general who was a born fighter.

On the evening of November 9, 1863, ten days before he was scheduled to deliver an address at the Gettysburg battle-field, Lincoln went to the theater. The play that night at Ford's Theatre, in Washington, was *The Marble Heart*, starring John Wilkes Booth. Lincoln watched the production from the presidential box. John Hay, the president's secretary, later complained that the performance seemed tame and uninspired. It would not be the last time Lincoln and Booth would meet at Ford's Theatre.

Chapter 4

THE WAR DRAGS ON
BOOTH'S PLOT THICKENS

*O*ne frozen January evening in 1865, Booth and his old friend, Samuel Knapp Chester, wandered the streets of New York City together. Chester had never been happier to see Booth. Chester was an actor, and times had been tough for him. He hoped that the successful Booth would include him in his next stage tour. It became apparent, however, that Booth had more on his mind than the theater. He spoke of "a new speculation" that Chester believed might be another business venture, such as the Pennsylvanian oil investments Booth had made the previous summer. Was his old friend going to invite him to share in this latest money-making scheme?

After they visited several saloons and oyster houses, Booth finally paused as they strolled up Fourth Street and spoke what was on his mind. His "speculation," to Chester's utter shock, was a conspiracy to capture the leaders of the U.S. government, including President Lincoln himself. Booth wanted to turn the captives over to the Confederate government, which would exchange them for southern prisoners of war. Once the southern prisoners were returned, the Confederacy would have enough men to continue fighting the war. As Chester stared in wild-eyed disbelief, his old friend invited him to join his conspiracy.

Chester told Booth he would have no part of the plot, but swore he would not betray him. Convinced he could count on Chester's silence, Booth parted from him and disappeared into the night.

What made one of America's most successful actors decide to kidnap the president? The reasons are not entirely clear, even today. Perhaps the answers lie both in Booth's twisted mind and the discouraging state of the South in the second half of 1864.

Military Stalemate

Early in 1864, the North seemed to be on the verge of final victory. Nearly two and a half years of war had exhausted the South's resources and its soldiers. Confederate General Robert E. Lee no longer seemed unbeatable after his defeat at Gettysburg. With Grant now in command of the Union's Northern Army, the final showdown between these two giants seemed to be approaching, with Grant emerging as the likely victor.

But that's not what happened. In May, Lee and Grant met head on in two major battles in northern Virginia—at what has come to be called "the Wilderness," and at Spotsylvania. Both battles were bloody and fierce, and there was no clear winner.

Grant telegraphed Chief of Staff General Henry Halleck and said "I...propose to fight it out on this line if it takes all summer."

But June proved no better than May. In a major assault at Cold Harbor, just north of Richmond, Union troops failed to move Lee's army. Grant advanced on the railroad center of Petersburg, south of Richmond, in a siege that would last nine long months. Meanwhile, Lee boldly sent troops north to attack Washington, hoping Grant would divide his forces to protect the capital.

President Lincoln went to see the fighting outside the city and became the only president under enemy fire while in office. Lincoln was under political fire, as well. His failure to oversee a decisive victory since Gettysburg, almost a year earlier, was making him extremely unpopular. Many northerners wanted to end the war quickly through peaceful negotiation. They were tired of the war and sickened by the heavy cost that the country was paying in human lives. If Grant or his lieutenants didn't win a major battle before November, Lincoln's chances of re-election looked grim indeed.

A Secret Meeting

John Wilkes Booth was facing a crisis of his own as summer approached. Although he was adored by the theater-going public and enjoyed one successful production after another, he seemed more anxious to earn the approval of the Confederacy and its

Booth was one of the country's most successful stage actors in the early 1860s.

scouts in the North. They appreciated his efforts at gathering military information and passing it along, but Booth wanted to do more.

In late May 1864, Booth finished his last star engagement in Boston. It was the end of his acting career, except for a few isolated performances. In early July, he met with Confederate secret agents at a Boston hotel. Whether the idea of capturing Lincoln originated with Booth or the agents is not certain. What is certain, is that by the time he met with Confederate agents in Montreal, Canada, three months later, a plan was in place. The agents gave him $1,500 to pay for the scheme. Booth later deposited the money in a bank on his return to Washington.

The Fall of Atlanta

One reason the Confederate government may have encouraged Booth's rather fantastic plot was that, by the fall of 1864, the situation had become desperate. Any plan to turn the tide of war was worth considering.

In August, Union Rear Admiral David G. Farragut entered the harbor of the city of Mobile, on the coast of Alabama, with a naval squadron. When he was told that Confederate torpedoes were floating in the harbor, Farragut is said to have cried the now-famous words, "Damn the torpedoes! Full steam ahead!" He quickly overcame enemy ships and seized the city of Mobile, cutting off the port—and the South—from much-needed supplies.

At the same time, General William Tecumseh Sherman and his troops were in Tennessee, and would soon be in Georgia's capital of Atlanta. Known as "the granary of the Confederacy," Atlanta was the storehouse for the South. Sherman once wrote confidently that "its capture would be the death knell of the Confederacy."

The ruins of Atlanta, after the Union's victory there in 1864.

The Confederates fought courageously under the leadership of General John B. Hood, but they gradually gave way under the attack of the Union army. Atlanta fell in early September.

Here at last was the victory that Lincoln needed. The North regained its fighting spirit, and in November, Lincoln was re-elected by a majority. He was the first president to win a second term since Andrew Jackson more than 30 years earlier.

The Conspiracy Takes Shape

The summer before Lincoln was re-elected, Booth began to put his plan for kidnapping the president into action. The first men he recruited for his conspiracy were two old friends from his school days—Samuel Arnold and Michael O'Laughlen. Both had served as Confederate soldiers from Maryland, and both were less intelligent than Booth. He was careful to choose no one for his conspiracy who might threaten his leadership. As in one of his stage productions, he would be the only star.

The plan he presented to his friends was not an impossible one. During the summer, Washington City, as it was then called, was unbearably hot. The Lincolns escaped the heat by moving to a modest cottage on the grounds of the U.S. Soldier's Home, on the outskirts of the capital. On many working days, Lincoln made the 4-mile commute to and from the White House either on horseback or in a carriage, with only a few men guarding him. It would not be difficult for a group of determined men with arms to overpower the guards and capture Lincoln. The conspirators would then take the president south through Maryland and on to the Confederate capital of Richmond, Virginia.

Booth probably picked John Surratt because of his familiarity with the region. Surratt was a Confederate messenger who knew every back road between Washington and Richmond. He would be invaluable in helping the group make an escape from the city. His mother, Mary Surratt, ran a boardinghouse where the conspirators could meet without arousing suspicion.

David Herold, a young man of little experience, also knew the back roads out of Washington. But his main attraction was his worship of Booth and his boyish enthusiasm for the plot.

George Atzerodt was a depressed, hard-drinking German who painted carriages for a living. His main strength was that he had a boat on the Potomac River and regularly ferried Confederate spies across it. The boat would be necessary to cross the river as the conspirators made their escape south.

The last of the principle players to join Booth was the quiet but moody Lewis Powell. Since Booth had last seen him, Powell had joined the Confederate Army and then deserted. Now, to avoid capture, he called himself Lewis Paine. When he met Booth by chance in Baltimore, Paine agreed to join the conspiracy. Strong and violent, he was completely loyal

George Atzerodt

to Booth. Paine also had a terrible sense of direction, however, and was easily confused by Washington's maze of streets.

As the summer passed and Lincoln no longer went regularly to his cottage, Booth abandoned the idea of kidnapping him on the road. Instead, he told his partners, they would grab the president at the theater during a performance, tie him up, lower him to the stage in his chair, and escape out the stage door. Arnold and O'Laughlen were shocked by the foolishness of this new plan.

When Lincoln was re-elected in November, Booth was more determined to carry out his scheme. He told his friends that the president would soon proclaim himself king. He wrote a long letter addressed "to whom it may concern," in which he explained the drastic actions he was about to take:

> *Right, or wrong, God, judge me, not man.... All hope for peace is dead, my prayers have proved as idle as my hopes. God's will be done. I go to see, and share the bitter end....*

My love (as things stand today) is for the South alone. Nor,
do I deem it a dishonor in attempting to make for her a
prisoner of this man, to whom she owes so much of misery.
If success attends me, I go penniless to her side.

Booth signed the letter "a Confederate, doing duty upon his own responsibility." He left the letter with his sister, Asia, in Philadelphia, possibly during their last meeting in February 1865.

Sherman's March

While Booth was preparing to do what he saw as his duty, Union General Sherman was grimly doing his. Both men wanted to end the war and were ready to employ unusual methods to do so. Having conquered Atlanta, Sherman and his troops burned the city nearly to the ground. Then, instead of chasing Hood's fleeing Confederate soldiers, Sherman began a march across Georgia to the sea, burning practically everything along his route. His plan was to strike the supply lines that kept the Confederates going— the farms in the Georgia countryside. Such a plan would not only drain the South of its resources, but break the spirit of the people.

Sherman's men took whatever food and goods they needed and destroyed what was left. Sherman's famous "march to the sea" took four weeks. That period of time would be re-membered bitterly by southerners for generations to come. On December 21, when Sherman reached the city of Savannah, on the coast, he sent Lincoln this telegram: "General Sherman makes the American people a Christmas present of the city of Savannah with 650 heavy guns and 25,000 bales of cotton."

Having left Georgia in ashes, Sherman next turned north and proceeded to do the same to the Carolinas before linking up with Grant in Virginia. The end of the war truly seemed near.

Before 1864, most wars in Europe and North America were fought and won on the battlefield. All that changed with General William Tecumseh Sherman's march from Atlanta to the sea.

The Civil War was, in a real sense, the first modern war in world history. For the first time, railroads played a major part in moving troops and supplies. The telegraph made communications faster than ever before. Modern factories turned out weapons and other instruments of war at a rate never seen before. Steamships, and even submarines, called "ironclads," were engaged in warfare.

Sherman understood the importance of this new technology of war and set out on his famous march to destroy the enemy by cutting off its line of supplies and communications.

"The arsenal, railroad, depots, storehouses, magazines, public property, and cotton…are today destroyed," wrote a soldier in Sherman's party. "There is not a rail upon any of the roads within twenty miles of Columbia [Georgia] but will be twisted into corkscrews before the sun sets."

Such tactics were meant to destroy not only the means of war, but the very spirit of the Confederacy, already tiring of a fight it was rapidly losing. As cruel as his actions may seem to us today, Sherman's reasons were intelligent. He knew this destruction would end the war sooner and save perhaps thousands of lives on the battlefield.

William Tecumseh Sherman

Sherman's tactics would later be adopted by men and women of the twentieth century. War as a contest between two armies on a field would give way to a total war of country against country, in which no-one—soldier or civilian—was safe.

The Conspirators Stumble

Booth and his gang would have to move fast or there would be no Confederacy left to receive the kidnapped president. In mid-January all was in place to kidnap Lincoln during a performance at Ford's Theatre, but the president never showed up. The conspirators met again a while later in Washington. Booth arranged an elaborate dinner in a private room at a restaurant. At the meeting, O'Laughlen and Arnold told Booth that his idea of capturing Lincoln in a theater, where there would be hundreds of witnesses, was absurd. Arnold insisted they change their original plan and grab the president while he was going for a carriage ride in the suburbs. The others agreed this was a more practical approach, and Booth, for once, gave in to their wishes. The men quietly waited for an opportunity to carry out their new plan.

Two weeks after their meeting, it was announced that Lincoln would attend a performance of a play at a soldier's hospital just outside the city. The conspirators quickly got ready to capture their prey. But again, at the last minute, the president changed his plans and didn't attend the performance.

Arnold and O'Laughlen had enough. They lost all confidence in Booth's ability to pull off the kidnapping scheme and told him so. Surratt was also ready to quit, and the next day he left for Baltimore. In one night, Booth lost half of his men.

The money that the southern agents had given him in Montreal was running out. Without income from the theater, Booth was nearly broke. He began to drink heavily. At the end of March, he went to New York to borrow money, which is why he looked up his old friend Sam Chester again.

Booth's appearance must have shocked Chester. Booth was pale and had little of his former self-confidence. He asked Chester for fifty dollars that Chester owed him. Then he told Chester that he had been at Lincoln's second inauguration and had stood very close to him. "What an excellent chance I had to kill the President... if I could."

For all Booth's talk, Chester may have decided that the plot was nothing but another example of Booth's active imagination. He must have breathed a sigh of relief when they parted, thinking that nothing more would come of Booth's conspiracy.

Chapter 5

TRAGEDY AT FORD'S THEATRE

*I*f someone had entered Ford's Theatre in Washington around six o'clock on the evening of April 14, 1865, he or she would have noticed a most peculiar sight. A handsome, well-dressed young man stood on the dimly lit stage of the 1,700-seat theater, holding a small pine board in one hand.

He quickly walked to the back of the empty theater and mounted the stairs to what was known as the "state box," where President Lincoln sat when he attended a performance. The man went through a first door that led into a passageway to the box, and he made a small hole in the plaster wall. It was just large enough so that one end of the board that he held could be inserted into the hole. The other end would rest against the door, wedging it shut. Then he took a small drill from his pocket and made a hole through a second door at the end of the passageway, which lead directly to the state box. The peephole gave him a perfect view of the rocking chair in the box and of the stage beyond it. The man then walked back downstairs, carefully studied the stage and seats on the lowest level one last time, and quietly left.

The young man who sneaked into the theater was not a thief. Nor did he make the peephole to get a free view of the performance that evening. He was the actor John Wilkes Booth, and his mysterious visit was a rehearsal for murder.

Surrender at Appomattox

In the several weeks since Booth's kidnapping plan fell apart, the Confederacy also crumbled. Sherman's march to the sea had achieved its purpose. The South was in a desperate state. In early April, Grant followed Sherman's example and took control of the railroad lines that supplied Richmond, Virginia.

Confederate troops fled the southern capital. Lee tried to join forces with General Johnston in North Carolina, but Grant blocked the way. When Grant sent a letter calling on Lee to surrender, the Confederate general came to the grim conclusion that "there is nothing left for me to do but to go and see General Grant, and I would rather die a thousand deaths."

The historic meeting took place on April 9, in a farmhouse at the tiny settlement of Appomattox Court House. The owner of the house, Wilmer McLean, had moved to Appomattox after his earlier house had been bombarded during the first battle of Bull Run. At least there would be no bullets this time.

Grant, dressed in his dirty private's (ordinary soldier's) coat, looked more like a loser. And Lee, dressed immaculately in his gray uniform, appeared every inch the conqueror. Both men conducted themselves with dignity and warmth.

Lee surrenders to Grant at Appomatox Court House.

Grant was generous in his terms. At Lee's request, he even allowed the Confederate soldiers to keep their horses for the spring planting many would soon be doing back home. Almost four years to the day after Fort Sumter was fired upon, the Civil War was over.

"I'll Put Him Through"

Two days after Lee surrendered, Lincoln delivered a speech on the White House grounds. Among the large crowd that turned out to hear him were Booth, Herold, and Paine. Booth was furious when Lincoln talked about the former slaves who would now become citizens in the South. "Now by God!" he said later.

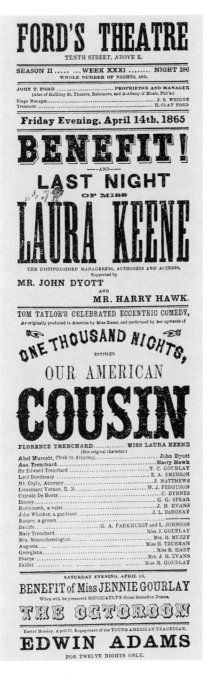

A copy of the program that was found in the president's box.

"I'll put him through. That is the last speech he will ever make."

With no Confederacy left to receive a captured Lincoln, Booth's desperate thoughts began to turn from kidnapping to murder. The assassination of the president and other government leaders would, Booth reasoned, throw the government into confusion and allow the South to rise again. If he himself died in the attempt, he would die a glorious death. All Booth needed was the opportunity. It came on April 14, Good Friday.

"The President and his Lady will be at the Theatre this evening," the afternoon papers announced. Booth only heard the news by chance that afternoon while chatting with his friend Harry Clay Ford as he picked up his mail, which was held for him at Ford's Theatre.

Booth was excited, but hid his surprise. There was much to be done, and only a few short hours to do it all. He rented a good horse to use in his escape from the theater and arranged a meeting with the remaining gang members to go over their assignments. Lincoln was to be accompanied to the theater by General Grant. Booth planned to assassinate them both.

At his hotel room, Booth drank some brandy. Perhaps he thought about the words he had written in a letter to his mother only the night before:

Dearest beloved Mother

I have always endeavored to be a good and dutiful son.... But dearest Mother, though I owe you all, there is another duty. A noble duty for the sake of liberty and humanity due to my Country.... I have not a single selfish motive to spur me on to this, nothing save the sacred duty, I feel I owe the cause I love, the cause of the South.... And should the last bolt strike your son, dear Mother, bear it patiently and think at the best life is but short, and not at all times happy....

Come weal or woe [good or bad fortune], *with never ending love and devotion you will find me ever your affectionate son,*

John

About eight o'clock in the evening, Booth met with his three co-conspirators for the last time in a hotel just a block from Ford's Theatre. Each received his gruesome assignment for the evening. Paine would murder Secretary of State William Seward, who was at home recovering from a carriage accident. Herold would accompany Paine and lead him safely out of the city after Paine committed the deed. Atzerodt was to kill Vice-President Andrew Johnson in his hotel room. Although Atzerodt protested that he had not agreed to commit murder, Booth wouldn't listen to him. Booth himself would kill the president.

The president's assassin didn't know that Grant would escape him. He had already refused the president's invitation. He and his wife were on their way to New Jersey to be with their children. It was actually Grant's wife, Julia, who had decided the matter. Julia didn't like the thought of an evening with the temperamental Mary Lincoln.

The conspirators would meet up later at the Navy Yard Bridge, or, if that didn't work, at Surrattsville, in Maryland. There, Mary Surratt owned a tavern, where the men had hidden weapons and ammunition.

On to Ford's Theatre

The Lincolns were late for the theater. It seemed no one but the president wanted to go. Robert Lincoln, his eldest son, had just arrived home from months of serving on General Grant's staff and said he needed a good night's sleep. Mrs. Lincoln had a headache and wanted to stay home, too. When her husband said he wouldn't go without her, she dutifully decided to make the effort. They stopped to pick up Major Harry Rathbone and his fiancée, Clara Harris—their guests for the evening in place of the Grants.

When the four arrived at the theater, the first act of the play was already underway. The action stopped as they entered, and the Lincolns were applauded. The play was a silly comedy called *Our American Cousin*. It was just the kind of mindless entertainment that made the president forget his troubles.

Booth was familiar with the play, having acted in it many times himself. He chose the moment he would strike carefully. It would be in the third act, during one of the play's biggest laughs. The laughter would hide the sound of the gunfire. And since there would only be one actor onstage at that time, Booth could more easily escape from the president's box via the stage.

As the performance progressed, Booth wandered restlessly between the theater and the Star Saloon, next door. Backstage workers and other theater people were not suspicious of his wandering. They knew him well and were happy to see him, though one actress later commented on how pale he had looked.

The Fatal Shot

At just past ten o'clock, Lincoln felt chilled and put on his long woolen overcoat. A few minutes later, Booth returned from the saloon for the last time and mounted the winding stairs to the seats near the state box. Under his coat he carried a small pocket pistol and a hunting knife. There should have been a guard in front of the door leading to Lincoln's box to stop the murderer. However, Washington police officer John F. Parker was not at his post. He was sitting nearby, enjoying the show with everyone else. Parker was a drunkard who had been dismissed from the force more than once. His very presence as Lincoln's bodyguard that night later led some people to believe that individuals with a lot more power than Booth were also involved in the conspiracy. But no concrete evidence has ever been produced.

Booth entered the passageway to the state box through the unguarded door and put the small pine board in place, which barred the door shut. He looked through his peephole in the second door, leading to the box, and saw Lincoln directly ahead, sitting in his rocker. He was concentrating on the action onstage.

The actor Asa Trenchard stood alone, about to deliver the last line of the scene. They were probably the last words that Abraham Lincoln ever heard.

"Don't know the manners of good society, eh?" teased the comic actor. "Wal, I guess I know enough to turn you inside out, old gal—you sock-dologizing old mantrap!"

The audience roared with delight. On cue, Booth opened the door and drew his tiny pistol. He pointed the barrel of the gun inches from the back of Lincoln's head and squeezed the trigger. The noise of the gunshot was lost in all of the laughter. Lincoln jerked his right arm as he was struck, and then

Booth assassinates President Lincoln.

collapsed in his seat, unconscious. The half-inch-wide bullet had smashed into his skull above his left ear and was wedged behind his left eye.

Seeing her husband slumped over, Mary Lincoln screamed. Major Rathbone turned and saw a man's figure emerge from a cloud of gunsmoke. The major tried to grab the assassin. Booth dropped the pistol, which had no more bullets, and attacked Rathbone with his knife. He missed his chest but made a deep cut in his arm.

Booth then grabbed the state box railing and swung over it in a 10-foot leap to the stage. His jump was not simply for dramatic effect. He could not expect to leave the way he had come and escape capture. It should have been an easy jump for the athletic young actor, but Rathbone made a grab for his coat, throwing Booth off balance. One of Booth's boot spurs caught in the presidential decorations on the outside of the box, and he landed awkwardly on his right foot. When he landed, a bone above his right ankle snapped.

Having given his most dramatic performance, Booth could not exit without making more of the moment. He stared out at the confused audience, waved his knife, dripping with Rathbone's blood, and cried, *"Sic semper tyrannis!"* It was a Latin phrase

Booth lands on the stage, almost losing his balance.

that meant, "Thus ever to tyrants," and it was the motto of the state of Virginia.

Then Booth limped offstage and slashed with his knife at the house manager, who tried to block his way. Booth rushed into the alley behind the theater, knocked down a boy who was patiently holding his horse for him, and rode into the night. (A man named Edwin Spangler had been holding his horse earlier.)

A Second Attack

Meanwhile, across town, the rest of the conspiracy was quickly coming apart. Atzerodt, true to his character, spent the evening getting drunk in a series of saloons and never went near Vice President Andrew Johnson's hotel. Paine, however, had a stronger character. Herold led him to Secretary of State Seward's home in Lafayette Square and waited outside. Paine entered the house, pretending to deliver medicine to the patient. When one of Seward's sons became suspicious and tried to stop him, Paine drew a revolver. The weapon wouldn't fire, so he beat Seward's son with it.

Paine then broke into Seward's sick room with a knife in his hand. Seward was wearing an iron brace around his neck to help his jaw heal from his injuries in the carriage accident. The brace saved his life. Paine only managed to slash his face three times before Seward fell out of bed. By then, another son and Seward's nurse were in the room and pulled the would-be assassin away from his victim. Paine fled the house.

Once he was safely outside Seward's house, Paine discovered that Herold was already gone. The youth had panicked when he heard the commotion inside and went looking for Booth. Paine was on his own. He mounted his horse and promptly got lost in Washington's maze of darkened streets.

It is hard to imagine that Abraham Lincoln was not always as beloved and respected as he is today. Within hours of his death, however, newspaper editors across the country were pulling out negative editorials and cartoons poking fun at the president and replacing them with eulogies.

It isn't surprising that Lincoln was hated in the South. But as the president boldly exercised the great power of a wartime leader, his popularity dropped in the North as well. Newspapers criticized him for suspending the *writ of habeas corpus*, a law stating that no citizen could be held in prison unless he or she was formally charged with committing a crime. As a result of the suspension, many southern sympathizers were imprisoned.

Democrats wanting to make peace with the South condemned Lincoln for energetically pursuing the war. Radical Republicans and influential blacks were disappointed in Lincoln for not making slavery a central issue early in the war.

With his death, all this animosity toward Lincoln was forgotten. The president was seen as a martyr to the Union cause. Some preachers even compared him to Jesus Christ, pointing out that he was murdered on Good Friday, the anniversary of Christ's crucifixion.

Today Lincoln is considered our greatest president, and rightly so. During the terrible ordeal of the Civil War, he worked tirelessly to preserve the Union. His speeches and other writings are among the finest

Abraham Lincoln

expressions of what our American democracy should be. In attempting to kill a hated tyrant, John Wilkes Booth helped to create a beloved saint.

A Dying President

Back at Ford's Theatre, the scene was one of utter panic. Rathbone, bleeding heavily from his arm, managed to take down the board wedged against the door and let in the first person on the scene, Dr. Charles Leale. The doctor examined the wound and could tell at once that the president would never recover. As Rathbone's fiancée, Clara Harris, tried her best to comfort Mary Lincoln, several doctors joined Leale and debated where to take the dying president. It was decided he would never survive the relatively long journey back to the White House. Instead he was carried on a crude stretcher to a boardinghouse across the street from the theater.

Lincoln was gently placed in a bed in a back room on the first floor. His tall frame was too long for the small bed, and he had to be laid down diagonally.

The death watch over the president lasted all night. About 90 politicians and other important people passed in and out of the tiny room. Secretary of War Edwin Stanton, who had not been targeted for death that night, soon arrived and took immediate charge. He barked orders left and right in a next-door room, at one point even ordering soldiers to "take that woman out of here" when Mary Lincoln started crying uncontrollably.

At 7:22 A.M., the waiting came to an end. The president breathed his last breath and was still. He had never once regained consciousness from the moment the bullet struck him.

Sometime later, it was learned that the bed Lincoln died in had been used only a month before by his assassin. While visiting an actor friend who lived at the boardinghouse, John Wilkes Booth had taken an afternoon nap on that very bed.

JOHN WILKES BOOTH AND THE CIVIL WAR

Chapter 6

FINAL CURTAIN

A little before eleven o'clock on the evening of April 14, 1865, a lone rider dressed in black approached the Navy Yard Bridge that spanned the Anacostia River, leading travelers out of Washington. An armed watchman stopped the rider and asked him to identify himself.

With no attempt at trickery, the horseman said his name was Booth. The watchman, Sergeant Silas T. Cobb, explained that he was under orders not to let anyone pass over the bridge after nine o'clock without special permission. Booth claimed he had been in Washington for the day on business and now needed to get home to Maryland. He had not known of the curfew.

Cobb thought a moment and then allowed Booth to continue on. When he was later questioned about letting the most wanted man in the country slip through his hands, he replied, "I thought he was a proper person to pass—and I passed him."

A few minutes later, he also allowed another rider to pass, a "Mr. Smith," who was probably no other than David Herold, trying to catch up with his leader. Booth and Herold did meet up, sometime before midnight.　⌐

Two Fugitives

The two fugitives rode to Surrattsville and the Surratt tavern to pick up the weapons they had left there earlier. The proprietor of the tavern was John Lloyd, who rented the establishment from Mary Surratt. Lloyd was drunk when they arrived, which may explain why he hardly reacted when Herold announced that he and Booth had assassinated President Lincoln. Lloyd gave Herold two rifles, ammunition, a pair of binoculars, and a bottle of whiskey. Booth got rid of his rifle because it was too heavy to carry. He drank the whiskey, though, to numb the terrible pain of his broken leg.

Booth knew he couldn't make it across the Potomac River with his leg being so painful. He needed immediate medical attention, and the only doctor he knew in the area was a 40-year-old gentleman farmer named Samuel Mudd. He had met Mudd a few months before, while he was looking around the area for escape routes.

Although he needed Mudd, Booth didn't trust him. He disguised himself with fake whiskers and a scarf pulled up around his face so the doctor wouldn't recognize him.

The two men arrived at Mudd's farmhouse near Bryantown, Maryland, about four o'clock in the morning. Herold explained that Booth had broken his leg in a fall from his horse. Mudd asked no further questions and put Booth's leg in a splint—a device that protects a broken bone. He let the injured man sleep in an upstairs room for what remained of the night and

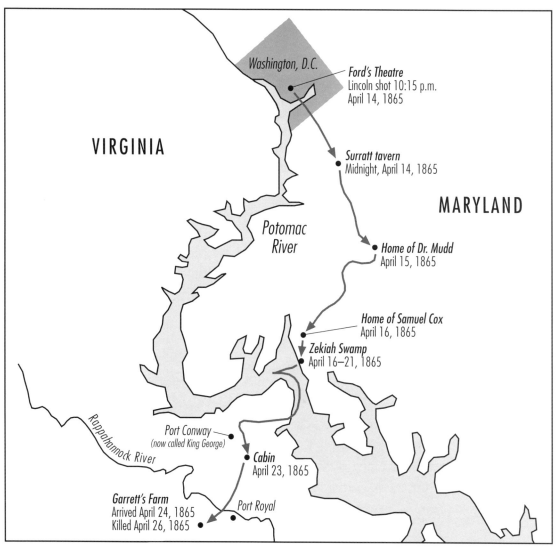

Booth's espape route. Lincoln's assassin was on the run for 12 days before he was caught.

had breakfast with Herold, who struck him as a rather foolish and immature young man.

Before leaving in the morning, Booth asked for a razor and shaved off his mustache. Mudd gave him a pair of crutches and sent him on his way. Whether he recognized Booth or not may never be known for certain, but Dr. Mudd would live to regret what he seemed to believe was a simple act of compassion.

Herold and Booth now rode to the home of a man Booth believed they could count on for help. He was a Confederate sympathizer named Samuel Cox, who happened to be the wealthiest man in the county.

Booth made no secret of who he was and what he had done. Cox was shocked. He wouldn't report Booth to the federal soldiers who were looking for him, but he didn't want to have him under his roof for very long, either. He contacted his foster brother, Thomas Jones, who had helped Confederate spies across the Potomac River during the Civil War. Jones felt more sympathy for Booth and his situation than Cox did. He agreed to help the two fugitives until they could safely cross the Potomac into Virginia.

Six Days in a Swamp

Jones hid the men in a small clearing of pines in Zekiah Swamp, a 15-mile stretch of desolate wilderness. Cold, miserable, and still in almost constant pain, Booth had one gleaming hope that kept him going. He felt certain that once he was across the Potomac and in Virginia, he would be safe from harm. The South would make him their hero and protect him from the Yankees who were hunting him.

When Jones brought him the newspapers he hungered to read, that hope died. Booth couldn't believe his eyes. He was called a mad killer in the South as well as in the North. Even Jefferson Davis and Robert E. Lee spoke out against Booth's deed.

Booth would not admit to any regrets about killing Lincoln, however. "I can never repent it," he wrote in his diary, "though we hated to kill. Our country owed all her troubles to him, and God simply made me the instrument of his punishment.... I care not what becomes of me. I have no desire to outlive my country."

But he would not sit and wait to be captured. Hearing soldiers moving nearby, and fearing that the horses would be noticed, Booth asked Herold to take the horses out into the water and shoot them.

After six days, Jones decided it was safe for them to move on. He led them to the Potomac River, showed them where to cross in order to reach Virginia, and gave them a rowboat for the journey. He agreed to take eighteen dollars from Booth, which was the cost of the rowboat, but nothing more. Days earlier, he could have turned the assassin in for a reward of $100,000, but he never considered it.

"God bless you my dear friend, for all you have done for me," Booth said in farewell. It was one week since the fateful night at Ford's Theatre.

A Nation in Mourning

While Booth was hiding in a Maryland swamp, the capital and the nation were mourning his victim. On Easter Monday, two days after he died, Lincoln's large, lead-lined coffin was carried into the White House's East Room, where it was on display to the public. When the White House doors opened Tuesday, the line of people was over a mile long. A raised platform, called a "catafalque," was specially built for the occasion.

Wednesday the funeral service for the first U.S. president to be assassinated was held in the White House. Mary Lincoln, too upset to attend, remained upstairs in her room during the service. The sermon was delivered by Lincoln's pastor, Dr. Phineas Gurley of the Methodist Episcopal Church. He spoke of "that dark hand of the assassin, which smote our honored, wise and noble President, and filled the land with sorrow."

After the service, a solemn procession accompanied Lincoln's coffin down Pennsylvania Avenue to the Capitol, where Lincoln lay in state for further public viewing. About 40,000 people marched in the procession, including generals, politicians, and ordinary citizens. Particularly moving was the sight of Washington's black citizens, dressed in their Sunday finest, and the Union veterans, some of them limping along on crutches.

"The grandeur and sadness of it all was indescribable," wrote authors Dorothy and Philip Kunhardt. "Every face in line was solemn—and most were streaked with tears."

All day Thursday, Lincoln lay in state in the Capitol's rotunda, the large room beneath the dome-shaped ceiling. On Friday, the coffin was loaded onto a special train that would carry it on a

About 40,000 people marched in President Lincoln's funeral procession.

1,700-mile journey back to Lincoln's home of Springfield, Illinois, where he was to be buried. The journey took nearly a week. The train stopped at every station so people could see their president one last time. Full-scale funerals were held in 12 cities along the way.

Closing In

The nation's grief soon turned to fury at the men responsible for this vicious act. Secretary of War Stanton, like some revengeful angel, brought all the power of the government to bear on the hunt for the assassin and his assistants. Even though they backed out of Booth's final plan, Surratt, O'Laughlen, and Arnold were identified as members of the conspiracy. Someone reported seeing Surratt in Elmira, New York, the day Lincoln died. But Surratt quickly fled north to Canada.

On Monday, April 17, O'Laughlen gave himself up in Baltimore, and Arnold was picked up in Virginia. Both men swore they had nothing to do with the assassination plot and were only a part of the earlier kidnapping scheme.

While detectives questioned Mary Surratt and her daughter at the Surratt boardinghouse, a man carrying a shovel came to the door and said he had been hired to dig a ditch. It was Lewis Paine, who had spent the last three days hiding in a treetop. His story might have worked, but Mrs. Surratt had poor eyesight and didn't recognize the man who used to live in her boardinghouse. She said she had hired no ditch digger. The unlucky Paine was questioned by the detectives and later identified as Seward's attacker.

Atzerodt, who had drifted to Germantown, Maryland, was arrested there at his brother's house on Thursday. The next day, agents picked up Dr. Mudd, who emphatically denied that he knew he was treating John Wilkes Booth.

David Herold

On that same day, both Booth and Herold were completely lost on the Potomac in their little rowboat, unable to find the Virginia shore.

"After being hunted like a dog through swamps, woods, and last night...with every man's hand against me, I am here in despair," Booth wrote during his ordeal. "Tonight I try to escape these blood hounds once more. Who can read his fate. God's will be done. I have too great a soul to die like a criminal."

Booth and Herold finally reached the Virginia shore in the early morning of April 23. The two men got a ride on a wagon that took them to the home of another wealthy southerner, Dr. Richard H. Stewart, who was a cousin of Robert E. Lee. Stewart refused to let them stay under his roof and allowed them only enough time to eat a meal in his kitchen before sending them on their way.

Booth was so insulted by the way he was treated, that he wrote Stewart an angry note. The letter, with its proud tone, was typical of Booth. Even while running for his life, he stopped to respond to a personal injury. In a final grand gesture that he could hardly afford, Booth enclosed $2.50 for his meal.

Dear Sir: Forgive me but I have some little pride.... I was sick and tired, with a broken leg, in need of medical advice. I would not have turned a dog from my door in such a condition.... Be kind enough to accept the enclosed two dollars and a half (though hard to spare) for what we have received.

Yours respectfully,
Stranger

These were the last words Booth ever wrote and may have saved Stewart from punishment at the hands of the law.

Booth's Final Act

Ironically, the two fugitives spent the night at the humble cabin of a former slave. The next day, a young man drove them by wagon to the town of Port Conway. There they waited for a ferry to take them across the Rappahannock River to Port Royal, a small community southeast of the city of Fredericksburg. As they waited, three ex-Confederate soldiers showed up to take the same ferry. Herold, ever the boy, boasted, "We are the assasinators of the President." The soldiers were impressed. One even asked Booth for his autograph. They agreed to help the men find a place to stay in Port Royal.

The first house wouldn't have them, but they received a friendlier reception at the farm of Richard Garrett. The soldiers and the fugitives convinced Garrett that Booth and Herold were ex-Confederate soldiers. The Garretts were a large family, and for the next 24 hours, Booth and Herold enjoyed a pleasant break from their lives as fugitives. Booth was his old charming self, despite his exhausted condition. He played merrily with the children and flirted with Mrs. Garrett's unmarried sister.

But then reality returned, as a troop of federal soldiers rushed by on horseback. Thinking they had been found, Booth and Herold pulled out their weapons and ran for the woods. The soldiers were on their trail, but they were actually going to the next town to find the three ex-Confederate soldiers who were traveling with them. Richard Garrett was shocked by Booth's and Herold's behavior and began to question them about their true identities.

Suspecting the two men were criminal fugitives, Garrett told them they had to leave his home. He agreed, however, to let the two spend the night in an old barn used for drying tobacco. They were to be on their way by daybreak.

Mrs. Surratt and Dr. Mudd——Villains or Victims?

Of Booth's eight co-conspirators who were punished for the death of President Lincoln, two may well have been innocent of any crime.

Mary Surratt ran the Washington boardinghouse that the group used as a meeting place. She also owned the tavern in Maryland where they sometimes met and eventually hid their weapons. But whether she was ever a part of their plot, or even knew it existed, remains in doubt. By most accounts, she was a good-hearted, religious woman, who favored the South. Her misfortune was that she had a son who came under John Wilkes Booth's fatal spell.

Much of the evidence against Surratt was given in her trial by Louis Weichmann, a boarder and friend. Weichmann, a man who could not be trusted, was promised a job by Secretary of War Stanton for his cooperation.

The morning Mary Surratt was to hang, her daughter, Anna, attempted to see President Andrew Johnson to stop the execution. Two senators prevented her from ever reaching Johnson. It is interesting that both men later committed suicide.

Dr. Mudd's story had a happier ending, but he, too, was punished for his connection with Booth. He was sentenced for life to Dry Tortugas Prison, off Key West, Florida, along with Arnold, O'Laughlen, and Edwin Spangler. (Spangler watched Booth's horse before Booth escaped from Ford's Theatre.)

Conditions at the prison were miserable, and in August 1867, an epidemic of yellow fever, a very serious disease, broke out. As the epidemic spread, the prison doctor died. Dr. Mudd took his place, saving many lives at the risk of his own. The prison officials were so grateful to Mudd that they appealed to President Johnson to pardon (officially forgive) Mudd. The president did so in February 1869, along with Arnold and Spangler. O'Laughlen had died of yellow fever during the epidemic.

Spangler was also dying, of tuberculosis. Mudd invited him to live at this home in Bryantown and cared for him in Spangler's final days. In light of his compassionate behavior, it seems too bad that Samuel Mudd is remembered today only for aiding an assassin. He inspired the expression, "his name is mud," which refers to someone in a state of shame.

Mary Surratt

Meanwhile the soldiers had tracked down one of the ex-Confederates at a nearby hotel. Holding a gun to the man's head, they demanded to know where Booth was. They got the answer they were looking for.

The soldiers arrived at the Garrett farm about midnight. When Garrett didn't cooperate, they threatened to kill him. One of Garrett's sons said Booth and Herold were in the barn. The soldiers fanned out and surrounded it.

With no possibility of escape, Booth demanded the soldiers let him have a fighting chance. The commander of the troop had no patience with Booth's demands. He had orders to take the assassin alive, and he had every intention of doing so. He threatened to burn the barn unless the two men came out and surrendered immediately. Herold took the offer. Booth called him a coward but didn't stop him.

The "stage" was his alone now, and Booth wanted a heroic ending. The barn was set afire and the flames rose up, illuminating Booth behind the spaces between the barn boards. Although the soldiers had strict orders not to fire, Sergeant Boston Corbett did anyway, striking Booth in the neck with one bullet. He later said God had directed him to fire his gun. History is sometimes strange. Booth had earlier given the same reason for killing Lincoln.

The bullet cut Booth's spinal chord, and he dropped to the ground, unable to move his legs or arms. The soldiers dragged him out of the barn and placed him on the farmhouse porch. For hours, as the barn burned down, Booth lay on the porch, dying. "Tell my mother I died for my country," he whispered at one point to his captors.

The body was sewn in a horse blanket and taken back to Washington. Booth was secretly buried beneath the floor of a government warehouse to prevent an angry public from abusing

The barn at Garrett's farm, where Booth hid, was set on fire.

his corpse. At the same site, the other conspirators would soon be tried by a military court.

Justice was swift and harsh. Herold, Paine, Atzerodt, and Mary Surratt were sentenced to hang on July 6, and they were executed the next day. O'Laughlen, Arnold, and Dr. Mudd were sentenced to life imprisonment. Edwin Spangler was sentenced to six years of hard labor. John Parker, Lincoln's guard, who might have prevented this tragedy, received no official blame. He served as a Washington police officer for another three years.

A Dark Legacy

Among American political assassins, John Wilkes Booth occupies a unique place. Most successful and would-be assassins were losers or loners. Booth was neither. He had a successful career on the stage, was well liked, and had many friends. Whether he was mentally unbalanced remains a question. Certainly Booth's hatred of Lincoln was shared by many southerners.

Booth's assassination of Abraham Lincoln at Ford's Theatre remains the most dramatic and far-reaching crime in American history. If Lincoln had lived, the Reconstruction period of re-organizing and rebuilding that followed the Civil War might have turned out differently. The same might have been true of the history of the South.

Andrew Johnson, who became president after Lincoln, was a southerner. He wanted whites to have most of the power in the South, and he was against giving freed slaves all of the basic rights enjoyed by white people. He was opposed by Republicans in Congress who wanted full rights for all blacks. In the end, new laws were passed to protect former slaves. However, the bitter feelings among white southerners prevented blacks from becoming equal citizens for many years. Lincoln could have balanced the needs of both white and black southerners and perhaps avoided much of the turmoil of Reconstruction.

As for Booth, the mysteries remain. His writings, published together for the first time in 1997, reveal a complicated man, who could love with the same passion that fueled such hate. The Civil War itself may have been in part responsible for Booth's desperate act. As the editors of his collected writings observe, "He could not endure the outcome of one of history's greatest wars, and there was a kind of desperate pain in him that only death could mend."

Chronology

The Life of John Wilkes Booth

1821	Booth's father, Junius Brutus Booth, arrives in America from England.
May 10, 1838	John Wilkes Booth born at the Booth family farm near Bel Air, Maryland.
1852	Junius Booth dies; family rents Baltimore home and returns to farm.
1855	In Baltimore, John Wilkes Booth gives first important theatrical performance.
1858	Joins stock company in Richmond, Virginia, and establishes himself as a leading actor.
1859	Joins Virginia militia briefly and is present at the hanging of John Brown at Harpers Ferry.
1860–63	Tours the country as leading actor; begins working as smuggler and secret agent for the Confederacy after war breaks out.
May 1864	Completes last star engagement in Boston.
October 1864	Talks with Confederate agents in Montreal, Canada, about plot to kidnap President Lincoln.
November– December 1864	Plans kidnapping conspiracy with six others.
April 14, 1865	Shoots President Lincoln during a performance of *Our American Cousin* in Ford's Theatre.
April 15, 1865	Lincoln dies at 7:22 A.M. in a boardinghouse across the street from Ford's Theatre.
April 26, 1865	Booth is shot by federal troops in a burning barn near Port Royal, Virginia, and dies several hours later.
July 7, 1865	Four of Booth's co-conspirators are hanged; three others receive life sentences.

The Life of the Nation

1820	Missouri Compromise passed by Congress admits Missouri into the Union as a slave state and Maine as a free state; compromise bans slavery "forever" from all territory north of 36°30′ north latitude.
1846–1848	Mexican War ends in a U.S. victory.

1850	The Compromise of 1850 brings California into the Union as a free state; part of compromise is Fugitive Slave Act, requiring all citizens to return runaway slaves to their masters.
1854	Kansas-Nebraska Act allows the residents of each new territory to decide for themselves whether to allow slavery within their borders.
1857	The U.S. Supreme Court hands down *Dred Scott* decision, denying slaves any rights as U.S. citizens.
1859	Abolitionist John Brown fails to capture arsenal at Harpers Ferry, Virginia; he is condemned for betraying his country and is hanged.
November 1860	Republican candidate Abraham Lincoln is elected sixteenth president of the United States.
December 1860	South Carolina becomes first southern state to secede from Union.
April 12, 1861	Confederate artillery fires on Fort Sumter in Charleston Harbor, setting off Civil War.
July 21, 1861	South wins a surprise victory at the first battle of Bull Run (Manassas).
September 17, 1862	Battle of Antietam is single bloodiest day of Civil War and a costly victory for North.
January 1, 1863	President Lincoln signs Emancipation Proclamation, freeing all slaves in Confederate states.
July 1–3, 1863	The battle of Gettysburg is major defeat for South.
September 1864	General William Tecumseh Sherman takes Atlanta.
November 1864	Lincoln re-elected to second term as president.
November–December 1864	Sherman conducts "march to the sea" from Atlanta to Savannah, Georgia.
April 9, 1865	Lee surrenders to Grant at Appomattox Court House, officially ending Civil War.
April 15, 1865	Lincoln dies at 7:22 A.M.

Glossary

abolitionist Someone who worked to put an end to slavery in the United States.

assassin Someone who murders a political leader or other well-known person.

blockade A blocking off of a place by military force in order to keep people and supplies from entering and leaving.

Confederacy The 11 southern states that seceded from the Union in 1861 and 1862 and formed their own government.

conspiracy A secret plot or plan to commit a wrongful or unlawful act.

conspirators Members of a conspiracy.

fugitive A person who is running away, often from the law.

gentry Refined and wealthy people.

jackstraws Literally, straws used in a game. In Whitman quote, empty-headed people.

Reconstruction The period in American history from 1865 to 1877 during which the southern states of the former Confederacy were reorganized and readmitted to the United States.

sentenced Informed of legal punishment.

territory A region of land not admitted as a state but having its own government.

Underground Railroad The escape route to the North for runaway slaves.

Source Notes

Chapter One

Page 9: "He had to plod, progress slowly step by step…" Asia Booth Clarke. *John Wilkes Booth: A Sister's Memoir.* Jackson, MS: University Press of Mississippi, 1996, p. 33.

Page 10: "His feelings were ardent…" Ibid., p. 36.

Page 11: "We must trample this law under our feet." James M. McPherson. *Battle Cry of Freedom.* New York: Oxford University Press, 1988, p. 82.

Page 12: "trying to starve respectably by torturing the barren earth." Clarke, p. 71.

Page 14: "His face shone with enthusiasm…" Ibid., p. 77.

Chapter Two

Page 15: "I saw John Brown hung…" John Rhodehamel and Louis Taper, eds. *'Right or Wrong, God Judge Me': The Writings of John Wilkes Booth.* Urbana, IL: University of Illinois Press, 1997, p. 60.

Pages 18–19: "Once-Twice- the impromptu battering ram thundered…" Edward White. "Eyewitness at Harpers Ferry." *American Heritage*, February 1975, p. 96.

Page 19: " [a] saint [who] would make the gallows glorious like the Cross." David Wallachinksy and Irving Wallace. *The People's Almanac.* Garden City, NY: Doubleday, 1975, p. 180.

Pages 20–21: "he wanted to be loved of the Southern people…" Clarke, p. 77.

Page 22: "This government cannot endure, permanently half *slave* and half *free*." *The World Book Encyclopedia.* Chicago: World Book, Inc., 1986, Vol. 12, p. 278.

Page 23: "I am a northern man…" Rhodehamel and Taper, p. 55.

Chapter Three

Page 24: "Each was what the other was not." Louis J. Weichmann. *A True History of the Assassination of Abraham Lincoln and of the Conspiracy of 1865.* New York: Alfred A. Knopf, 1975, p. 40.

Page 28: "the leading actor in the greatest and stormiest drama known..." John Carey, ed. *Eyewitness to History.* Cambridge, MA: Harvard University Press, 1987, p. 372.

Page 28: "The Pride of the American People..." Stanley Kimmel. *The Mad Booths of Maryland.* Indianapolis, IN: Bobb-Merrill Co., 1948, p. 172.

Page 33: "More than half a mile their front extends..." Frank Aretas Haskell. "The Third Day at Gettysburg." *American Heritage*, December 1957, p. 38.

Chapter Four

Page 37: "I...purpose to fight it out on this line if it takes all summer." *The World Book Encyclopedia*, Vol. 4, p. 488.

Page 38: "Its capture would be the death knell of the Confederacy." Captain B.H. Liddell. "Sherman—Modern Warrior." *American Heritage*, August 1962, p. 103.

Pages 41–42: "Right, or wrong, God, judge me, not man..." Rhodehamel and Taper, pp. 124–125.

Page 42: "General Sherman makes the American people a Christmas present..." *The World Book Encyclopedia*, Vol. 4, p. 492.

Page 43: "The arsenal, railroad, depots, storehouses, magazines..." Carey, p. 370.

Page 44: "What an excellent chance I had to kill the President..." Rhodehamel and Taper, p. 14.

Chapter Five

Page 46: "There is nothing left for me to do..." Douglas Southall Freeman. *Lee of Virginia.* New York: Charles Scribner's Sons, 1958, p. 201.

Pages 47–48: "Now by God! I'll put him through..." Rhodehamel and Taper, p. 15.

Page 48: "The President and his Lady will be at the Theatre this evening." Carey, p. 372.

Page 49: "Dearest beloved Mother..." Ibid., pp. 130–131.

Page 51: "Don't know the manners of good society, eh?" Jim Bishop. *The Day Lincoln Was Shot.* New York: Scholastic, 1970, p. 208.

Chapter Six

Page 57: "I thought he was a proper person to pass—and I passed him." Robert E. Jakoubek. *The Assassination of Abraham Lincoln.* Brookfield, CT: Millbrook Press, 1993, p. 48.

Page 60: "I can never repent it…" Rhodehamel and Taper, p. 154.

Page 61: "God bless you, my dear friend, for all you have done for me," Gene Smith. "The Booth Obsession." *American Heritage*, September 1992, p. 114.

Page 61: "that dark hand of the assassin…" Dorothy Meserve and Philip B. Kunhardt. "Assassination!" *American Heritage*, April 1965, p. 32.

Page 62: "The grandeur and sadness of it all was indescribable…" Kunhardt, p. 33.

Pages 63–64: "After being hunted like a dog…" Rhodehamel and Taper, pp. 154–155.

Page 64: "Dear Sir: Forgive me…" Ibid., p. 159.

Page 65: "We are the assassinators of the President." Smith, p. 115.

Page 67: "Tell my mother I died for my country." Leroy Hayman. *The Death of Lincoln: A Picture History of the Assassination.* New York: Scholastic, 1968, p. 101.

Page 69: "He could not endure the outcome of one of history's greatest wars…" Rhodehamel and Taper, p. 15.

Further Reading

Burns, Bree. *Harriet Tubman* (Junior World Biographies series). New York: Chelsea House, 1994.

Colver, Anne. *Abraham Lincoln: For the People* (Discovery Biographies series). New York: Chelsea House, 1992.

Dolan, Edward F. *American Civil War: A House Divided*. Brookfield, CT: Millbrook Press, 1997.

Jakoubek, Robert E. *The Assassination of Abraham Lincoln* (Spotlight on American History series). Brookfield, CT: Millbrook Press, 1993.

January, Brendan. *The Dred Scott Decision* (Cornerstones of Freedom series). Danbury, CT: Children's Press, 1998.

January, Brendan. *The Emancipation Proclamation* (Cornerstones of Freedom series). Danbury, CT: Children's Press, 1997.

Kent, Zachary. *The Civil War: A House Divided*. Hillsdale, NJ: Enslow, 1992.

Ray, Delia. Behind the Blue and Gray: The Soldier's Life in the Civil War. New York: Dutton Children's Books, 1991.

Reef, Catherine. *Civil War Soldiers* (African-American series). New York: Twenty-First Century Books, 1993.

Robertson, James I. *Civil War!: America Becomes One Nation*. New York: Knopf Books, 1992.

Web Sites

For quick facts on Booth and important people and places associated with him, go to:
http://www.aces.k12.ct.us/classweb/derby2/

For information on Booth's escape route (including maps and photographs), and links to information on his assassination, go to:
http://www.nps.gov/foth/escapjwb.htm

For information on Booth's last days, including Lincoln's assassination, Booth's escape, and his death, go to:
http://www.ibiscom.com/booth.htm

For eyewitness accounts on the chase and capture of Booth, go to:
http://home.att.net/-rjnorton/Lincoln73.html

For various links on Harriet Tubman's life, including her escape from slavery and her participation in the Civil War and the Underground Railroad, go to:
http://www.acusd.edu/-jdesmet/tubman.html

For more information on the *Dred Scott* decision, try:
http://www.arthes.com/gdg/causes5.html

To read Abraham Lincoln's first and second inaugural addresses, the Emancipation Proclamation, and the Gettysburg Address, go to:
http://libertyonline.hypermall.com/Lincoln/index.html

To take a tour of Abraham Lincoln's home in Illinois and learn more about his family and childhood, try:
http://www.nps.gov/liho/

For descriptions and summaries of the major conflicts of the Civil War, go to:
http://www.cr.nps.gov/abpp/abpp.html

The Library of Congress has information on the Civil War at:
http://www.loc.gov

For information on the battle of Gettysburg, including battle descriptions, area attractions, and maps, go to:
http:www.gettysburg.com

Index

Photo Credits

Cover and page 29: ©Corbis; pages 4, 18, 31, 33, 48, 52, and 68: ©North Wind Picture Archives; pages 10, 27, 37, 43, 47: ©Corbis-Bettmann; page 13: ©Corbis-Bettmann/UPI; pages 20, 25, 41, 53, 64, 66: ©Culver Pictures, Inc.; pages 21 and 39: Library of Congress; page55: ©Blackbirch Press, Inc.; page 62: National Archives.